29.95

CLEAN WATER

Published in the United States of America by Cherry Lake Publishing
Ann Arbor, Michigan
www.cherrylakepublishing.com

Content Adviser: Michael Rockett MS, Natural resources

Reading Adviser: Marla Conn MS, Ed., Literacy specialist, Read-Ability, Inc.

Photo Credits: © hxdyl/Shutterstock.com, cover, 1; © Biarstan/Shutterstock.com, 5; © Nikolay Gyngazov/Shutterstock.com, 6; © ktsdesign/Shutterstock.com, 8; © jaap posthumus/Shutterstock.com, 9; © Yuri Samsonov/Shutterstock.com, 10; © Take Photo/Shutterstock.com, 13; © baipooh/Shutterstock.com, 14; © Riccardo Mayer/Shutterstock.com, 16, 20; © Manuel Findeis/Shutterstock.com, 19; © guillermo_celano/Shutterstock.com, 22; © Jo Ann Snover/Shutterstock.com, 25; © Phonix_a Pk.sarote/Shutterstock.com, 26; © Volodymyr Tverdokhlib/Shutterstock.com, 28

Library of Congress Cataloging-in-Publication Data has been filed and is available at catalog.loc.gov

Cherry Lake Publishing would like to acknowledge the work of the Partnership for 21st Century Learning.
Please visit www.p21.org for more information.

Printed in the United States of America
Corporate Graphics

ABOUT THE AUTHOR

Ellen Labrecque has written over 100 books for children. She is passionate about being a friend to the environment and taking care of our planet. She lives in Pennsylvania with her husband, Jeff, and her two young "editors," Sam and Juliet. She loves running, hiking, and reading.

TABLE OF CONTENTS

CHAPTER 1

History:
Clean Water

Environmentalism is a big word. But its meaning is simple. Practicing environmentalism means being a friend of Earth and all its creatures. Environmentalists want to keep our air healthy, our land clean, and our water fresh. They want to take care of our plants and animals by making sure our planet remains a safe place to live. Some environmentalists focus on encouraging people to stop polluting. Others encourage people to **recycle**. One of the most important environmental jobs is to get everyone access to clean water.

The Story of Clean Water

Ninety-eight percent of Earth's water is salt water. We can't drink salt water. Animals can't drink salt water. We can't water

The ocean covers about 71 percent of Earth.

plants with salt water. This is why civilizations have always been built around fresh water sources such as lakes and rivers. All living things—animals, plants, and people—need fresh water to survive. Without fresh water, we couldn't fight off diseases, go to the bathroom, or digest our food.

Fresh water is our most important **natural resource**. It is a **renewable resource** because of rain. This means there is an unlimited amount. But we don't take care of it the way we should. Beginning in the 18th century, we started using machines and factories to make things. These factories dumped **waste** directly

Polluted water can cause fish to die.

into our waterways. Our bodily waste was dumped into the water, too. **Runoff** from construction sites also polluted water. All of this made some of our fresh water undrinkable. People would get sick when they drank it. But for a long time, we didn't know this. Finally in 1855, Dr. John Snow made an important discovery about our water supply.

Cholera

Snow was a medical doctor in England who believed that people were dying from the disease known as cholera because they were drinking unclean water. Cholera causes throwing up and diarrhea. People can die within hours of contracting it. At the time, people didn't have running water or even toilets. They used all the same water from pumps for drinking, cooking, and washing. Some of the water came from the Thames River, where people dumped waste and garbage. In 1854, a big breakout of cholera happened in Soho, a suburb in London. The disease killed 616 people. All the people who died had been drinking from the same pump. The pump came from a well that was right next to an area where people dumped their waste. Unfortunately, this was leaking into the well. After this pump was closed down, nobody else became sick and died. Scientists then

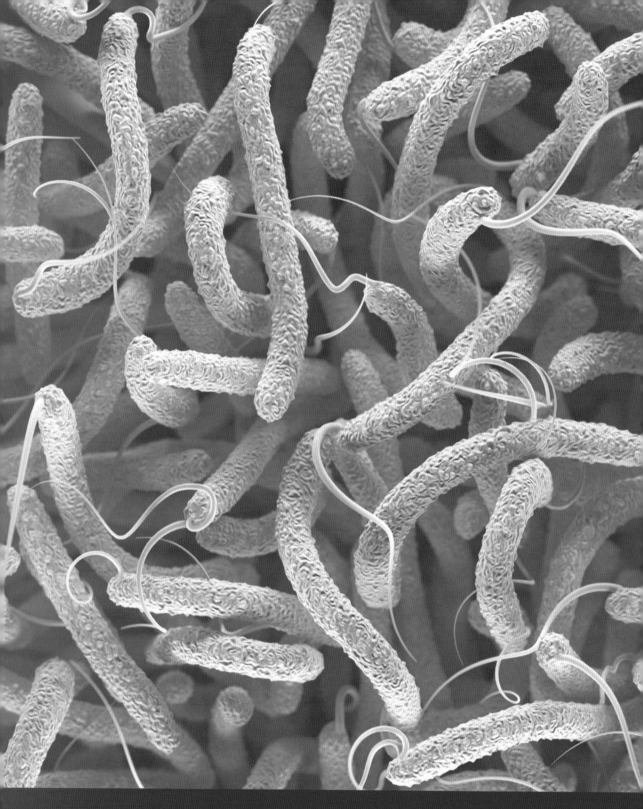

People can contract cholera from drinking polluted water.

Some people use water filters at home.

started to understand just how important a clean water source is.

People began looking for ways to guarantee clean water for everybody. In the 1890s, scientists began to put **chlorine** in the drinking water. The chlorine killed all the small germs that made people sick. This, along with the development of **filtration systems**, made clean water more available. In 1948, the United States passed the Federal Water Pollution Control Act. This act was the first one to force people to stop polluting rivers, lakes, and streams throughout the country. In 1972, the act was changed to the Clean Water Act, which is still enforced today. In 1974,

Many people in the United States can safely drink tap water.

the Safe Drinking Water Act was passed. This act made sure that the water coming out of our taps was safe to drink. Some studies have shown that before this act was passed, one-third of our tap water was unsafe.

Developing Questions

Water treatment plants exist all around the world. These plants treat wastewater from our toilets and make sure it's clean before it's returned to rivers and lakes. Reread the passage in this chapter. How important are water treatment plants? Why do we need them?

A close-ended question is a question that can be answered with a simple yes or no. An open-ended question is one that needs more thought when answering. The questions above are meant to be open-ended questions. They are meant to make you think about the importance of clean water, rather than just answering yes or no.

CHAPTER 2

Geography: Water Stress

The world **population** is increasing by about 80 million people a year. All these people need water to drink and to grow their food. Despite these rising numbers, our fresh water supply isn't growing. Countries fight over the rights to fresh water every day. In northern Africa, Egypt and Sudan fight for control over the Nile River. In the Middle East, countries like Turkey and Iraq fight for control of the Tigris and Euphrates Rivers.

Even with the limited amount of clean water, people are still polluting many of our sources. In some poor countries, 70 percent of garbage is dumped into waterways, including 2 million tons of human waste every day.

People continue to toss garbage into the oceans, rivers, and lakes.

In 2011, Thailand experienced severe flooding. Researchers believe it was caused by climate change.

Climate change may be also causing drought in some places and flooding in others. Long periods of drought dry up rivers and lakes, leaving people without water. Flash flooding leads to dirt and runoff overwhelming our water supply. The runoff makes fresh water undrinkable.

Africa

More than 1 billion people around the world don't have access to clean water. Over 330 million of these people live in sub-Saharan Africa. This area includes countries like Somalia and South Sudan, which are located south of the Sahara Desert.

Gathering and Evaluating Sources

Different types of maps show different things. A political map shows the borders of countries and states. Physical maps show landscape features, such as mountains and rivers. Some environmentalists use Water Scarcity Maps. These maps show areas of the world that are at risk due to lack of clean water. Check out www.wri.org/our-work/project/aqueduct to see these maps yourself.

Charity: Water is an organization that helps deliver safe drinking water to developing countries, like Africa.

Children die here every day from drinking dirty water. The rivers in this area, like the Zambezi in sub-Saharan Africa, are polluted, and there are very few water treatment plants to help clean up these waters. Most people do not have indoor plumbing—they go to the bathroom outside. And the well water that many people drink isn't clean.

Collecting Water

In many places in Africa, people spend hours walking miles to collect clean water every day. This leaves little time for kids to go to school and for adults to go to work. People try to steal water from others so they don't have to get it themselves. Organizations around the world are working to help people in Africa have access to clean water.

China

China has more than 21 percent of the world's population. But it only has 7 percent of the world's water supply. And many of its sources, like the Yangtze River, are polluted from chemical waste dumped from factories. China has been trying to build more water treatment plants around the country that clean this dirty water and make it drinkable again. It has also built sludge factories across the country. Sludge factories take the waste from the water treatment factories—called sludge—and turn it into clean energy to fuel cars. Before these factories were built, the sludge was dumped into **landfills**.

CHAPTER 3

Civics: Clean Water for Everybody

Everybody knows how important clean water is. But we may be taking it for granted. An average person in the United States uses 50 to 80 gallons (189 to 303 liters) of water each day. Some people use 2 gallons (7.5 L) just to brush their teeth. But there are ways you can use less water and make a difference. You can start by turning off the faucet when you are brushing your teeth. You can take shorter showers. You can also make sure you don't litter or pollute, especially into drains. This garbage can affect our fresh water sources, like lakes and rivers.

On a bigger scale, organizations around the world are working to keep our water clean and to make clean water more accessible to those who don't have it.

There are many ways we can help save and protect the environment.

Everyone around the world deserves clean water.

Schools for Clean Water

H_2O for Life is an organization that connects schools in the United States with schools in other countries, like Africa, that don't have clean water. By raising money, the US schools help the other schools create hand-washing stations, build new water wells, and make tanks that catch water.

National Ground Water Association

Groundwater is fresh water that flows underground in the soil and in the crevices of rocks. It accounts for 30 percent of the

Developing Claims and Using Evidence

The average US citizen uses 50 to 80 gallons (189 to 303 L) of water per day. This is more than any other country. In Africa, the average family uses just 5 gallons (19 L) a day. Do you think US citizens should try to cut back on their water use? Can you find evidence supporting this and evidence against this? Using evidence you find, form your own opinion about our country's water use.

People build wells into aquifers in order to pump out fresh groundwater.

world's fresh water supply. But this supply decreases year after year. Thirteen of the 37 largest **aquifers** in the world are considered at risk of becoming drained. The association works to protect these groundwater sources. It teaches people about the importance of keeping the groundwater clean as well as how to use it wisely and not waste it.

Top Five Countries with the Least Access to Clean Water

1. Somalia
2. Ethiopia
3. Madagascar
4. Papau New Guinea
5. Democratic Republic of Congo

CHAPTER 4

Economics: Funding for Clean Water

Scientists estimate that to bring clean water to the entire world, it would cost $10 billion a year. This sounds like a lot of money. But it is the same amount that Americans spend annually on pet food and Europeans spend annually on ice cream. If we did bring clean water to everybody around the world, this could save the lives of more than 2 million people who die every year from drinking unclean water.

Build More Desalination Plants

Desalination is the process of removing the salt from ocean water to make the water fresh and drinkable. As of 2015, about 300 million people get fresh water from more than 18,000

This is a desalination plant in the Caribbean.

These environmentalists are helping clean up an oil spill.

desalination plants around the world. More of these plants need to be built, but they cost as much as $1 billion per plant. And a lot of energy is required to keep these plants working.

Clean Up Aquifers

Groundwater supplies around the world are becoming more polluted from waste such as oil and gas seeping into the supply. China relies on its aquifers to supply 70 percent of its population with fresh drinking water. But aquifers in nine of every 10

Chinese cities are polluted. Cleaning these up would take a considerate amount of time and could cost a lot of money.

Build Water Wells

Digging wells can help people reach fresh groundwater that is as much as 600 feet (183 meters) below the surface. Countries in places like Africa need supplies such as drills, electricity, and fuel to get to this deep-water source.

Taking Informed Action

Do you want to help the world have clean water? There are many ways you can get involved and many organizations you can explore. Check them out online. Here are three to start your search:

- *Clean Water Action: Learn how you can protect our water and health.*
- *The Obakki Foundation: Find out ways you can help get clean water to people in Africa.*
- *Clean Waterways: Discover how you can keep water clean.*

Drinking clean water keeps us happy and healthy.

Make Water Pure

Sometimes rivers and lakes closest to people's homes are polluted. By using sand and clay filters, these waters can become clean again.

Clean Water Helps Save Money

More than half of the diseases in our world are caused by unclean water. It costs a lot of money to treat and help these people. In the United States alone, more than $500 million a year is spent on treating illnesses from unclean water.

Communicating Conclusions

Before reading this book, did you know how many people didn't have access to clean water? Now that you know more, why do you think this is an important issue? Share your knowledge about the world's water shortage and the importance of getting people clean water. Every week, look up different organizations that work toward getting everybody clean water. Share what you learn with friends at school or with family at home.

Think About It

There are more than 7 billion people living on Earth. It is estimated that by 2050, 9.7 billion people will be living here. Population growth and access to clean water are linked together. The more people on our planet, the more clean water we need to survive. Why do you think some countries struggle with getting clean water? Use the data you find in your research to support your argument.

For More Information

FURTHER READING

Ayer, Paula, and Antonia Banyard. *Water Wow! An Infographic Exploration*. Ontario: Annick Press, 2016.

Kallen, Stuart. *Running Dry: The Global Water Crisis*. Minneapolis: Lerner Publications, 2015.

Woodward, John. *Water*. New York: DK Publishing, 2009.

WEB SITES

Environmental Protection Agency
www.epa.gov/students
Find more information about the world's water crisis.

United States Geological Survey (USGS)
www2.usgs.gov/water
Learn all about water and where it comes from.

Water.org
www.water.org
This group works to bring clean water to everybody in the world.

GLOSSARY

aquifers (AK-wuh-furz) underground layers of rock, sand, or gravel that contain groundwater

chlorine (KLOR-een) an element used to purify or clean water

climate change (KLYE-mit CHAYNJ) a change in normal weather patterns over a long period of time

drought (DROUT) a period of dry weather

environmentalism (en-vye-ruhn-MEN-tuhl-iz-uhm) working to protect the air, water, animals, and plants from pollution and other harmful things

filtration systems (fil-TRAY-shun SIS-tuhmz) processes where water is passed through a device to make it clean

landfills (LAND-filz) large outdoor areas used to dump garbage

natural resource (NACH-ur-uhl REE-sors) something that can be used from nature such as land, forests, minerals, and water

population (pahp-yuh-LAY-shuhn) the number of people in one place

recycle (ree-SYE-kuhl) to break something down in order to make something new from it

renewable resource (rih-NOO-uh-buhl REE-sors) natural power, such as wind, that will never be used up and can be used again and again

runoff (RUHN-awf) water that flows off the land, carrying material from the soil with it, and into rivers and streams

waste (WAYST) a by-product of the body after it breaks down food and liquids

INDEX